NEW PROVIDENCE

A CHANGING CITYSCAPE

NEW PROVIDENCE

A CHANGING CITYSCAPE

SILVER BURDETT GINN

Needham, MA   Parsippany, NJ

Atlanta, GA   Deerfield, IL   Irving, TX   Santa Clara, CA

**SILVER BURDETT GINN**
A Division of Simon & Schuster
160 Gould Street
Needham Heights, MA 02194–2310

Illustrations in watercolor on board. Text set in Perpetua by Central Graphics, San Diego, CA. Designed by Nancy Ponichtera and Joy Chu

Simon & Schuster edition, 1996

2 3 4 5 6 7 8 9 10 BA 01 00 99 98 97 96

ISBN 0-663-59257-7

For Mrs. Ree Overton Fleming, whose support has nourished our efforts

— RONALD LEE FLEMING AND RENATA VON TSCHARNER-FLEMING

For Amy

— DENIS ORLOFF

With our special thanks to

Richard W. Cheek and J. A. Chewning, project consultants; Klaus Roesch, project designer; Beverlee Seronik Barnes, Catherine Evans, David Murray, and Tamar Rosenbloom, project researchers; Rosemary Jason, Russell Melies, Roberta Reeder, and Sharon Smith, project assistants; George E. Turnbull, design counsel

and to our advisory board

Elena Guilini, Richard S. Jackson, Jr., Franke Keefe, John Lees, Nellie Longsworth, Klaus Peters, Carole Rifkind, John Roll, Eduard Sekler, George E. Turnbull, Peter Vanderwarker, Charles G. I. Warner

and to Jörg Müller for the inspiration

1910 1935 1955

1970 1980 1992

Put the city up; tear the city down;
put it up again; let us find a city....

— CARL SANDBURG

1910

New Providence is thriving. Cobblestone streets bustle with activity—Model T Fords, streetcars, and horse-drawn carts carrying meat, milk, and ice. There is no concert in the bandstand today, but a crowd has gathered in the square in front of the Town Hall and the Tenebo County Courthouse. A fountain has been built in commemoration of Chief Tenebo, a Native American from a local tribe. The statue is about to be unveiled. Around the base of the fountain is an inscription: GOOD CITIZENS ARE THE RICHES OF A CITY.

New Providence's good citizens—women in long skirts and men in hats—buy fruit at the sidewalk stand in front of the grocery and most of their clothing and household items at Getz &

McClure's, the largest store in town. They shop for shoes and jewelry and office supplies and have supper at Gilman's or at the Butler House Cafe.

The rural hillsides surrounding the city are lush, with comfortable Victorian homes dotting the landscape and the Bloom mill and worker housing in the distance. The large red brick schoolhouse is attended by all school-age children in the region. A flock of birds flies peacefully overhead.

New Providence is filled with a typical jumble of late-nineteenth-century architectural styles: Gothic, Classical, and Romanesque revivals, Queen Anne and Italianate Victorians. Pictured here is the Colonel Fleming House, which was built in the late eighteenth century and is the last single-family home left on the square.

1935

As a mist rolls into New Providence, effects of the Great Depression are visible; the city has fallen on hard times. Gone is the bandstand from the courthouse square, where homeless men now huddle over trash can fires for warmth. A WPA sign publicizes the Works Progress Administration, a jobs program funded by the government. A line of jobless men waits for free bread outside the post office, and hoboes are taking a free ride out of the city on trains. Many buildings are in need of repair.

But even in times such as these, life goes on. A Charlie Chaplin movie is playing at the Strand Theater. A huge Coca-Cola advertisement goes up on the side of a building. A streetlight now controls automobile traffic. The Bloom mill—expanded before the stock market crash—is still in operation, the grocery has become a shoe store, and the dry goods store, a jeweler's. The Colonel Fleming House now accommodates three small businesses. Art Deco chrome and glass streamline some of the storefronts, contrasting with the older styles of the upper stories. A modern yellow apartment building squats on the hillside, while a biplane and a blimp cruise the skies.

A neoclassical granite post office has been constructed, revealing the train station in the distance.

The house at the end of Main Street has been replaced by a cottage-style gas station.

1955

Apostwar prosperity settles over New Providence, although there are signs that downtown is deteriorating.

The night sky glows with neon, Christmas lights, and lighted billboards advertising bread, used cars, and cigarettes. Part of the courthouse square is now paved with asphalt to make room for more and larger cars. Buses have replaced streetcars. Franchises like Rexall's and Woolworth's have moved into town, and the Alpine Motel attracts traveling businessmen. Walt Disney's *Lady and the Tramp* is playing at the Strand.

The elegant Butler House is now a liquor store and a boarding house for transients. Next to it, a

Victorian cast-iron building is being covered with prefabricated siding. Getz & McClure's has already been sheathed with stark metal grillwork and a currently popular style of lettering. Two of the small businesses in the Colonel Fleming House are boarded up. Behind it, a bland new building has been erected to house Monarch Insurance. The old slate roof of the Town Hall has been replaced by asphalt shingles. A fire is raging at the train station, while the citizens of New Providence go about their holiday shopping.

The nuclear age arrives: An air-raid siren has replaced the decorative ornament atop Town Hall, and the courthouse bears a fallout shelter sign.

The baby boom following World War II explains the new addition to the school-house. The surrounding hills are gradually filling up with the ranch-style and split-level houses of suburbia.

1970

By 1970, downtown New Providence is an uninspired jumble of old and new. To attract people from thriving suburbia, part of Main Street has been converted into a pedestrian mall, dominated by a harsh concrete fountain. But there is less traffic than ever in the city center, and fewer people actually live there.

A number of people in town today are gathered outside the courthouse, taking part in a protest march against the Vietnam War. Across the newly sunken and cemented square, a mugging is in progress. Graffiti mars the area, as do more and more billboards—advertising beer, cigarettes, whiskey, and an Army/Navy surplus store. The post office and several other buildings have been

An ordinary digital clock now hangs where there was once a quaint shoe sign, and the bank's classical architecture has recently been covered with mirrored glass.

The Butler House features trendy boutiques, a Day-Glo mural, and resident hippies. Space-age pavilions line the sidewalk.

demolished and turned into parking lots, the Bloom mill is for rent, and the train station tower remains burnt out.

The Alpine Motel is now a Holiday Inn, a Fotomat has opened, and the Beatles' *Let It Be* is playing at the Strand. A day school has opened, complete with colorful murals and giant toadstools. The Colonel Fleming House seems about to be rescued by a preservation group. Victorian homes in the hills are disappearing to make room for highways, look-alike suburban housing, and another addition to the school. In the afternoon sky, a jet flies over the increasing number of powerlines strung across the horizon.

1980

Ten years later, there are signs that downtown New Providence is sadly in need of recovery—
and also signs that help is on the way.

Chief Tenebo's statue has been vandalized; debris blows around its dry base and across the
square. Graffiti is everywhere, street lamps are smashed, and a police box has appeared. The
Colonel Fleming House has been moved across the street, but its placement does not look
permanent. In its old location are a Cor-Ten steel sculpture and Monarch Insurance's new highrise,
which bears no architectural relationship to the buildings around it.

But the streets seem more populated, and people are again living—even barbecuing—downtown in the new red brick infill structure next to McDonald's. The only billboard in town advertises health food and a cultural event. The old Strand Theater is being expanded into a Cultural Center. And although the Butler House has been all but abandoned, a sign shows that rehabilitation is being planned. A superhighway now cuts through the hillside, making downtown more accessible to summer holiday travelers. A large parking structure has been built, and well-tended plantings soften the mall.

A Feminist Health Center has replaced the Medical Offices, and New Providence has its first McDonald's.

Graffiti and rusted steel girders indicate that citizens' groups have so far been able to prevent further construction of a highrise office tower on the old post office site.

It is wisdom to think the people are the city ....

— CARL SANDBURG

1992

In the sunny afternoon sky a flock of birds heads back to its winter home. Below, people have returned to the city—living, shopping, working, playing. New Providence has never looked better. Sidewalk vendors sell their produce once more, and traffic again flows through handsomely paved streets. Buses are made to look like old-fashioned trolleys. Chief Tenebo has been restored, and the bandstand is back, a concert in full swing. Gone are graffiti, billboards, and harsh sculptures. Plants and fall flowers are everywhere—even the parking structure has been elegantly camouflaged.

All of the old building facades have been renovated, and the condition of most buildings is strikingly similar to what it was in 1910. The Town Hall's slate roof has been restored, and the air-raid siren is gone. Street furniture is comfortable and compatible with the architecture. The circular clock is back in front of the Butler House, now beautifully refurbished. An arcaded building where people live and work occupies the site of the controversial tower, serving as an entry into the restored train station, and an atrium full of plants softens the Monarch Insurance skyscraper. A Fitness Center has replaced the Feminist Health Center, and a film festival is in progress at the Strand Cultural Center.

The good citizens of New Providence have worked hard to make the city livable again—and true to its heritage.

The Colonel Fleming House has been carefully restored—not as a historical museum but as an outdoor restaurant.

New buildings and additions to existing structures have been designed to complement the medley of architectural styles in downtown New Providence.

New Providence, a small American city, will not be found on any map. It is the creation of a team of architectural historians and designers, and yet its fictional cityscape is truly authentic. The buildings, the signs, even the street furniture can be found somewhere in urban America. Almost every detail was discovered in old photographs and assembled by the design team at The Townscape Institute.

Baltimore, Maryland (McDonald's building and H_2O fountain); Binghamton, New York (courthouse lights); Boston, Massachusetts (church in center and 1970 concrete plaza); Brookline, Massachusetts (church); Cambridge, Massachusetts (signs); Chelsea, Massachusetts (storefront); Chicago, Illinois (metal awning on the Butler House); Cincinnati, Ohio (1987 City Identity System booth); Denver, Colorado (building across the street from courthouse in 1910); Eugene, Oregon (1970 modern concrete fountain); Flint, Michigan (1910 shoe sign and street awnings); Fresno, California (1970-80 sculptural clock tower); Garland, Utah (Bloom mill); Grand Rapids, Michigan (City Hall); Heber City, Utah (water tower); Junction City, Kansas (corner bank) ; Knoxville, Tennessee (billboard); Los Angeles, California (Getz & McClure building); Milwaukee, Wisconsin (suburban villas); Montclair, New Jersey (Colonel Fleming House); Montgomery, Alabama (Victorian cast-iron building); New York, New York (Butler House and train station); Portland, Oregon (fountain base); Richmond, Virginia (signs on Reiter's shoe store); Salem, Ohio (cornice on Main Street); San Diego, California (circular clock); Scottsdale, Arizona (parking structure with plantings); Staunton, Virginia (stained glass in McDonald's building); Syracuse, New York (layout of courthouse square); Topeka, Kansas (Alpine Motel sign); Townsend, Massachusetts (bandstand); Traverse City, Michigan (mansard roof on Butler House); Upper Sandusky, Ohio (horse fountain and pavilion); Waltham, Massachusetts (bench); Washington, D.C. (Masonic building); Westerville, Ohio (gas station); Wilkes-Barre, Pennsylvania (park outline); Wilmington, Delaware (1970 metal Main Street shelters); Winooski, Vermont (Main Street building).

Glossary

a·ban·don (ə ban′ dən) *v.* To leave empty. *They might abandon the old barn and never use it.*

ac·ces·si·ble (ak ses′ ə bəl) *adj.* Easy to get to. *The park is accessible from many different highways.*

ac·com·mo·date (ə käm′ ə dāt) *v.* To have enough room for. *The car can accommodate six people.*

ar·cade (är kād′) *n.* A passageway covered by an arched roof. *The building has an arcade on the top floor.*

ar·chi·tec·ture (är′ kə tek′ chər) *n.* A style or way of creating a building. *The architecture of the library shows that it was built long ago.*

com·mem·o·ra·tion (kə mem ə rā′ shən) *n.* In honor or memory of someone or something. *In commemoration of their grandparents, the children planted a garden.*

de·bris (də brē′) *n.* Scattered pieces of broken things and other rubbish. *Every day they collect debris from the park and put it in the garbage.*

de·te·ri·o·rate (dē tir′ ē ə rāt) *v.* To lose value. *The old car is beginning to deteriorate.*

fa·cade (fə säd′) *n.* The front of a building. *They paint the facade of the school every spring.*

graf·fi·ti (grə fēt′ ē) *n.* Pictures and words scribbled on objects in public places. *Red and orange graffiti cover the bus.*

harsh (härsh) *adj.* Rough, not pleasing. *One poster is beautiful, but the other is harsh.*

high·rise (hī′ rīz) *n.* A very tall apartment or office building. *She lives on the forty-third floor of the highrise.*

ho·bo (hō′ bō) *n.* A person who wanders from place to place and may have no home. *The family gives food to the hobo.*

lush (lush) *adj.* Covered with thick, healthy plants. *The garden is lush.*

mill (mil) *n.* A building where articles are made by hand or machine. *He works in a mill where clothing is made.*

ne·o·class·ic·al (nē ō klas′ ək əl) *adj.* A style of architecture that is new but based on an old classical design. *There are many neoclassical buildings in town.*

pre·fab·ri·cate (prē fab′ rə kāt) *v.* To make something in sections and then later put the parts together. *Our house was prefabricated in Florida and then assembled where we live in Ohio.*

pres·er·va·tion (prez ər vā′ shən) *n.* The act of preserving or protecting something so that it will keep for future generations to admire and understand. *The town committee is in charge of the preservation of public buildings.*

pros·per·i·ty (prä sper′ i tē) *n.* The condition of being wealthy and successful. *There is a lot of prosperity in the town because the people work hard.*

Vic·to·ri·an (vic tôr′ ē ən) *adj.* A style of architecture named after the English queen Victoria, which was popular over a hundred years ago. *They live in a beautiful, old Victorian house.*

van·dal·ize (van′ dal īz) *v.* To damage property. *They tried to vandalize the store, but guards kept them away.*

un·veil (un vāl′) *v.* Uncover. *As I unveil the statue, everyone sees how beautiful it is.*

tran·sient (tran′ shant) *n.* A person who moves from place to place. *He calls himself a transient because he lives in hotels.*

thrive (thriv) *v.* To grow. *Plants thrive in healthy soil.*

sub·ur·bi·a (sə bur′ bē ə) *n.* A name for a town or area that is near the edge of a large city. *They want to move from the city to suburbia, but they haven't chosen a town yet.*

sheathed (shēthd) *adj.* Covered. *To cover her arms, she sheathed them in long gloves.*

re·store (rē stôr′) *v.* To bring back to a former condition. *To restore the old house, they put in oil lamps instead of electric lights.*

ren·o·vate (ren′ ə vāt) *v.* To make new or like new. *After they renovate each old house, people move in.*

re·ha·bil·i·ta·tion (rē hə bil ə tā′ shən) *n.* A return to good condition. *After the rehabilitation, the school looked new.*

re·fur·bish (rē fur′ bish) *v.* To fix up, make like new again. *They will refurbish the old house before they move in.*